CONtexts

The Never Ending Sentence

Contexts

The Never Ending Sentence

Edited by Mary Stephenson
Design by Simon Heath
Artwork support by Rose Chapman

Sheena Best, Darren B, D. Brown, Damon Cooper, Ian Griffin, G. Jenkins, Simon Joyce, Scott Pratt, Steve Sanders.

The Contexts Project was funded by the Regional Arts Lottery Programme and HMP Channings Wood

Books from the Contexts series can be ordered at £5 per copy plus postage and packing from:

Writers in Prison Network Ltd.
P.O. Box 71
Welshpool SY21 0WP

Tel/Fax: 01938 811 355

PRISON LIFE

Hi! I'm Steve. I'm 28 years old and I'm doing a 2 year sentence at the Wood, being Channings Wood.

f this is your first time, don't worry or be afraid.

t makes it worse if you're afraid: people notice and take advantage of it.

Like always asking for your burn or units, I know from my first ime, so don't let people get you down. Find something to do. I did - matchstick modelling.

have made four boats, a plane, helicopter, picture frames and 've been asked if I can make a prison cell for this book that you re reading.

So don't be afraid! Make some friends even if you don't like hem. (They might not like you at first.)

So what? That's life.

f you are missing your wife and kids, have a visit. If you still miss them which I do, have a cry at night - who is going to know?

So what is there to be afraid of? (Nothing) nothing at all. So if ou are reading this book it means you're in prison, so use it. Go o the GYM, get a job: it's money, it might be the only money hat you get, if you don't have any sent in.

So the motto to this is, DON'T BE AFRAID.

BACK IN THE DAY

by Geoff Jenkins

When I first went to prison, I didn't realise how hard it was going to be Although I knew the basics, learnt from mates who had been in befor me, what I didn't know was how hard and frustrating my stay in prisor would turn out to be, due to my inability to read and write.

The first hurdle came in Reception, when I was given an informatio pack to read. This pack contained information on how I would get visits apply for letters to write home, the rules of the prison and what help wa on offer.

Things went downhill from Reception as nothing could prepare me fo the time I would spend locked behind the cell door - some 22 or 2 hours. Doing nothing, day in, day out, takes some doing. It was s unbelievably boring, other cons read from books, mags or papers, o wrote letters home to fill in the time, whilst I just lay on my bed starin at the ceiling.

At the end of the first week I had two letters off my family which I wa unable to read and a few important applications to fill in, but I couldn't I wasn't about to let on to anyone, or ask for help with reading an writing as I didn't want to look daft in front of the other cons. I'd als heard stories about other lads in my boat, who had asked other cons fo help with disastrous consequences. One lad I heard about asked a con t help with reading his letters, which he did, and then went round tellin everyone what was in the letters. I also heard about another lad wh asked for help with writing a letter home, the lad he asked wrote th letter for him but filled it with things that he shouldn't have, and thi caused all sorts of problems with his family.

By the end of my second week I knew I was in trouble and due to no being able to read and write, quite vulnerable to the predators tha roamed the landings of the jails. So I decided to seek help and believ me, that wasn't easy as I felt embarrassed and ashamed at the situation was in. But needs must. So I ended up on basic education and althoug at times I was pulling my hair out with frustration at the learning process which was a slow process, it had its rewards. I read my first book i prison, I now enjoy reading and have read many hundreds of book which has also helped me escape the boredom of prison and I've als started to get some exams behind me and all that.

Opposite is an example of what this passage of writing would look like to me before I was able to read and write.

ΒΑΧΚ ΙΝ ΤΗΕ ΔΑΥ

βψ Γεοφφ ϑενκινσ

Ωηεν Ι φιρστ ωεντ το πρισον, Ι διδν’τ ρεαλισε ηοω ηαρδ ιτ ωασ γοινγ το βε. Αλτηουγη Ι κνεω τηε βασιχσ, λεαρντ φρομ ματεσ ωηο ηαδ βεεν ιν βεφορε με, ωηατ Ι διδν’τ κνοω ωασ ηοω ηαρδ ανδ φρυστρατινγ μψ σταψ ιν πρισον ωουλδ τυρν ουτ το βε, δυε το μψ ιναβιλιτψ το ρεαδ ανδ ωριτε.

Τηε φιρστ ηυρδλε χαμε ιν Ρεχεπτιον, ωηεν Ι ωασ γιϖεν αν ινφορματιον παχκ το ρεαδ. Τηισ παχκ χονταινεδ ινφορματιον ον ηοω Ι ωουλδ γετ ϖισιτσ, αππλψ φορ λεττερσ το ωριτε ηομε, the ρυλεσ οφ the πρισον ανδ ωηατ ηελπ ωασ ον οφφερ.

Τηινγσ ωεντ δοωνηιλλ φρομ Ρεχεπτιον ασ νοτηινγ χουλδ πρεπαρε με φορ the τιμε Ι ωουλδ σπενδ λοχκεδ βεηινδ the χελλ δοορ – σομε 22 ορ 23 ηουρσ. Δοινγ νοτηινγ, δαψ ιν, δαψ ουτ, τακεσ σομε δοινγ. Ιτ ωασ σο υνβελιεϖαβλψ βορινγ, othep χονσ ρεαδ φρομ βοοκσ, μαγσ ορ παπερσ, ορ ωροτε λεττερσ ηομε το φιλλ ιν the τιμε, ωηιλστ Ι φυστ λαψ ον μψ βεδ σταρινγ ατ the χειλινγ.

Ατ the ενδ οφ the φιρστ ωεεκ Ι ηαδ τωο λεττερσ οφφ μψ φαμιλψ ωηιχη Ι ωασ υναβλε το ρεαδ ανδ α φεω ιμπορταντ αππλιχατιονσ το φιλλ ιν, βυτ Ι χουλδν τ. Ι ωασν τ αβουτ το λετ ον το ανψονε, ορ ασκ φορ ηελπ ωιτη ρεαδινγ ανδ ωριτινγ ασ Ι διδν τ ωαντ το λοοκ δαφτ ιν φροντ οφ the othep χονσ. Ι’δ αλσο ηεαρδ στοριεσ αβουτ othep λαδσ ιν μψ βοατ, ωηο ηαδ ασκεδ οτηερ χονσ φορ ηελπ ωιτη δισαστρουσ χονσεθυενχεσ. Ονε λαδ Ι ηεαρδ αβουτ ασκεδ α χον το ηελπ ωιτη ρεαδινγ ηισ λεττερσ, ωηιχη ηε διδ, ανδ thev ωεντ ρουνδ τελλινγ εϖερψονε ωηατ, ωασ ιν the λεττερσ. Ι αλσο ηεαρδ αβουτ ανοτηερ λαδ ωηο ασκεδ φορ ηελπ ωιτη ωριτινγ α λεττερ ηομε, the λαδ ηε ασκεδ ωροτε the λεττερ φορ ηιμ βυτ φιλλεδ ιτ ωιτη τηινγσ τηατ ηε σηουλδν’τ ηαϖε, ανδ τηισ χαυσεδ αλλ σορτσ οφ προβλεμσ ωιτη ηισ φαμιλψ.

Βψ the ενδ οφ μψ σεχονδ ωεεκ Ι κνεω Ι ωασ ιν τρουβλε ανδ δυε το νοτ βεινγ αβλε το ρεαδ ανδ ωριτε, θυιτε ϖυλνεραβλε το the πρεδατορσ τηατ ροαμεδ the λανδινγσ οφ the φαιλσ. Σο Ι δεχιδεδ το σεεκ ηελπ ανδ βελιεϖε με, τηατ ωασν’τ εασψ ασ Ι φελτ εμβαρρασσεδ ανδ ασηαμεδ ατ the σιτυατιον Ι ωασ ιν. Βυτ νεεδσ μυστ. Σο Ι ενδεδ υπ ον βασιχ εδυχατιον ανδ αλτηουγη ατ τιμεσ Ι ωασ πυλλινγ μψ ηαιρ ουτ ωιτη φρυστρατιον ατ the λεαρνινγ προχεσσ, ωηιχη ωασ α σλοω προχεσσ, ιτ ηαδ ιτσ ρεωαρδσ. Ι ρεαδ μψ φιρστ βοοκ ιν πρισον, Ι νοω ενφοψ ρεαδινγ ανδ ηαϖε ρεαδ μανψ ηυνδρεδσ οφ βοοκσ ωηιχη ηασ αλσο ηελπεδ με εσχαπε the βορεδομ οφ πρισον ανδ Ι ϖε αλσο σταρτεδ το γετ σομε εξαμσ βεηινδ με ανδ αλλ τηατ.

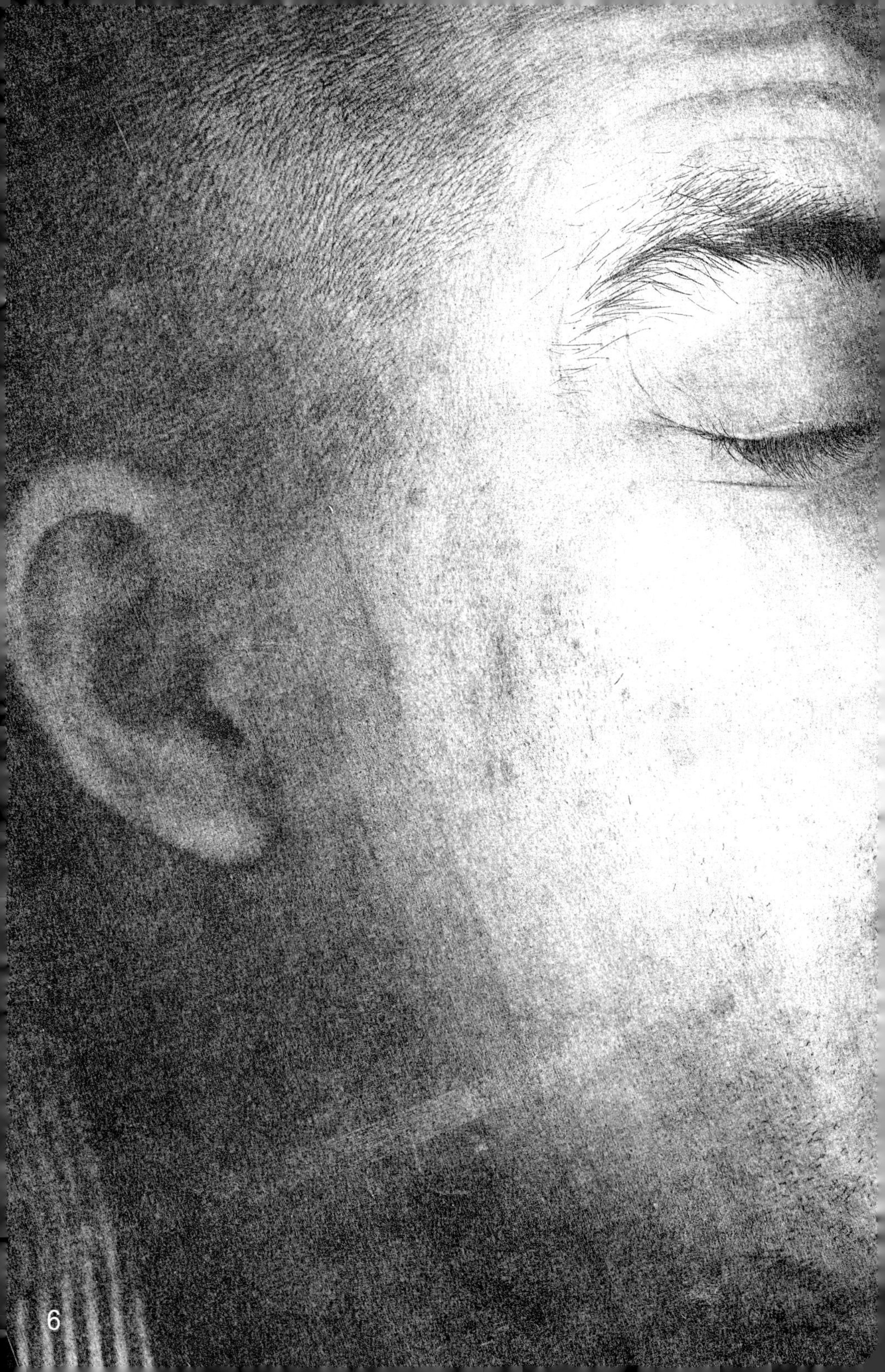

PeTTY RULES & what I think about them

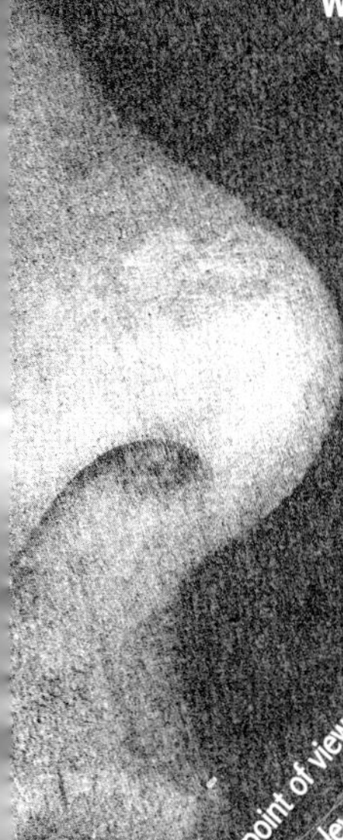

The point of view from my side - I know some rules are needed to help keep everything in order but some of these rules seem very petty as regards to level warnings for untidy cells. Who decides they are untidy, the officers or the person responsible? Both have different ideas as to the cleanliness and tidiness. Who sets standard of what we should be aiming at? When different officers and governors do cell inspections every person has their own set standard. I have seen one person given a level warning today for a bit of fluff in his cell. Two days before he was given a £4 canteen bonus for having a clean cell - canteen bonuses are given as an incentive to keep cells clean .What is the point when two days later you can get a level warning for an untidy cell? The warning is recorded on your records and if you get three level warnings you are put on basic. This to me isn't very fair. If an officer has a problem with an inmate because he's always causing problems and doesn't follow the rules, the officer may use this against him and put him on basic or get him shipped out to another prison to get him out of the way.

HOW TO SPOT A...

BULLSHITTER

The Bull shitter, he's been there, done that, got the T-shirt and makes up stories that aren't true.

Says any thing to make him look big, but no one likes him because he always tells lies.

biding my time

by Scott Pratt
FW5530

The inmate has just left prison after 11 years and has just missed the wagon...and starts thinking about the last eleven years.

The view from the wagon as he is taken to prison.

The prison gates

Just about to become like a bird caged for the first time and going through the process.

Getting his prison clothes and losing a bit of respect.

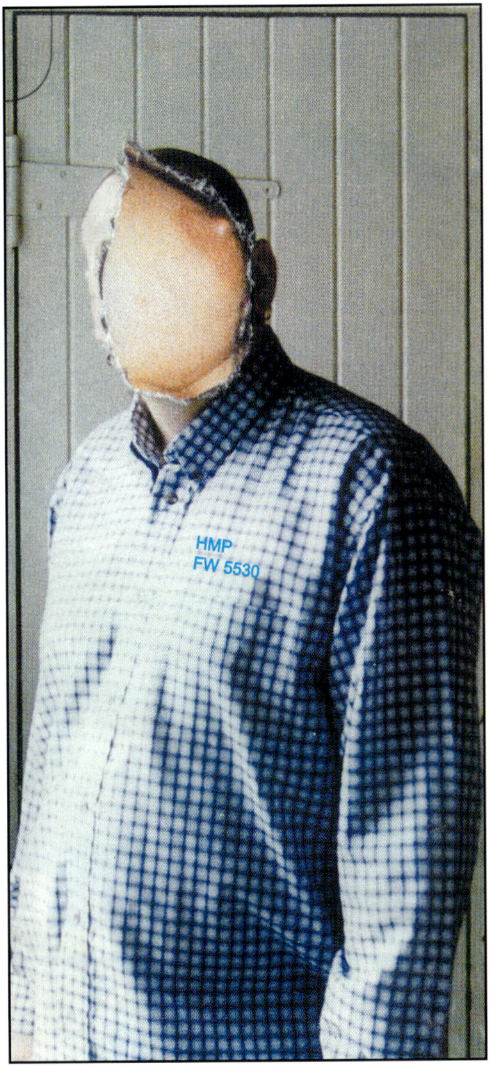

{feels a bit of a tit}

Sat in cell

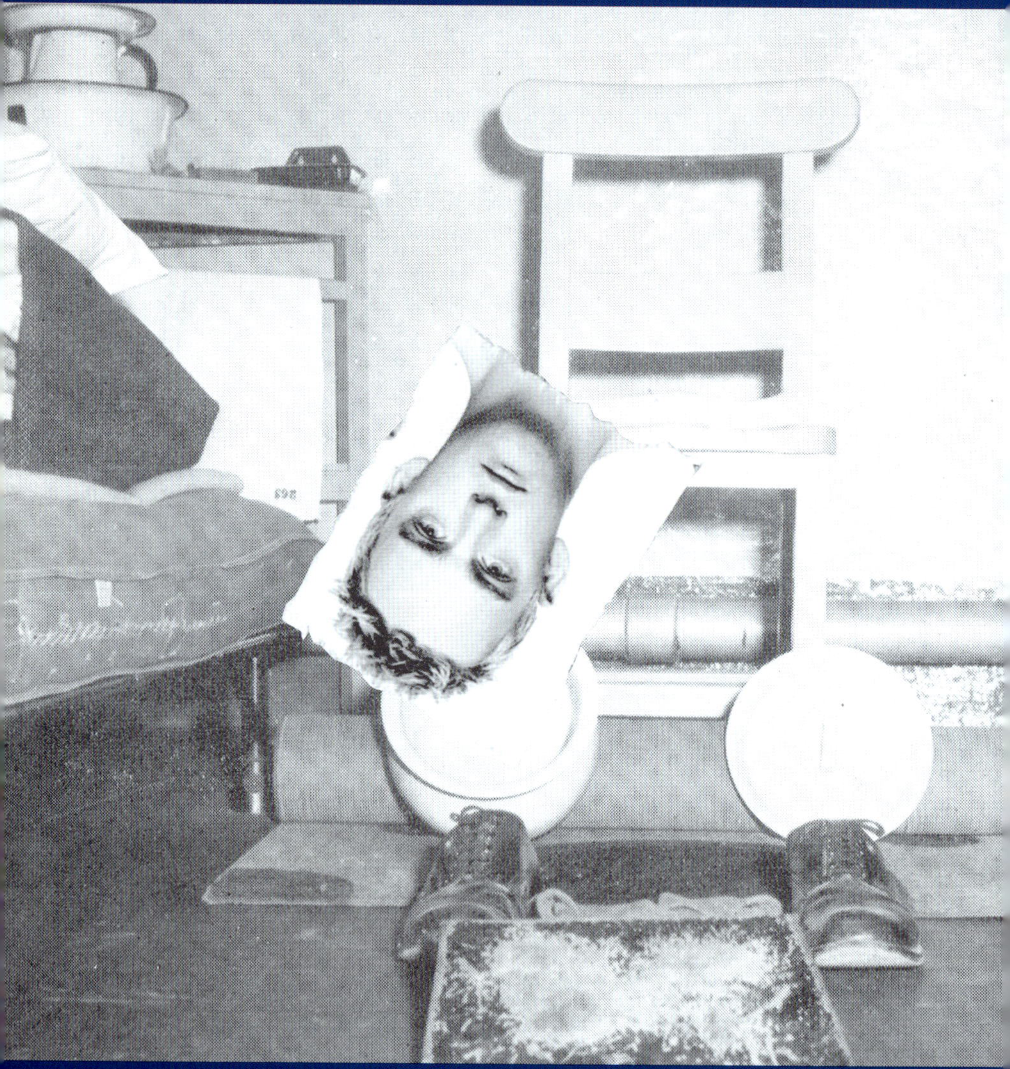

(feels like drowning)

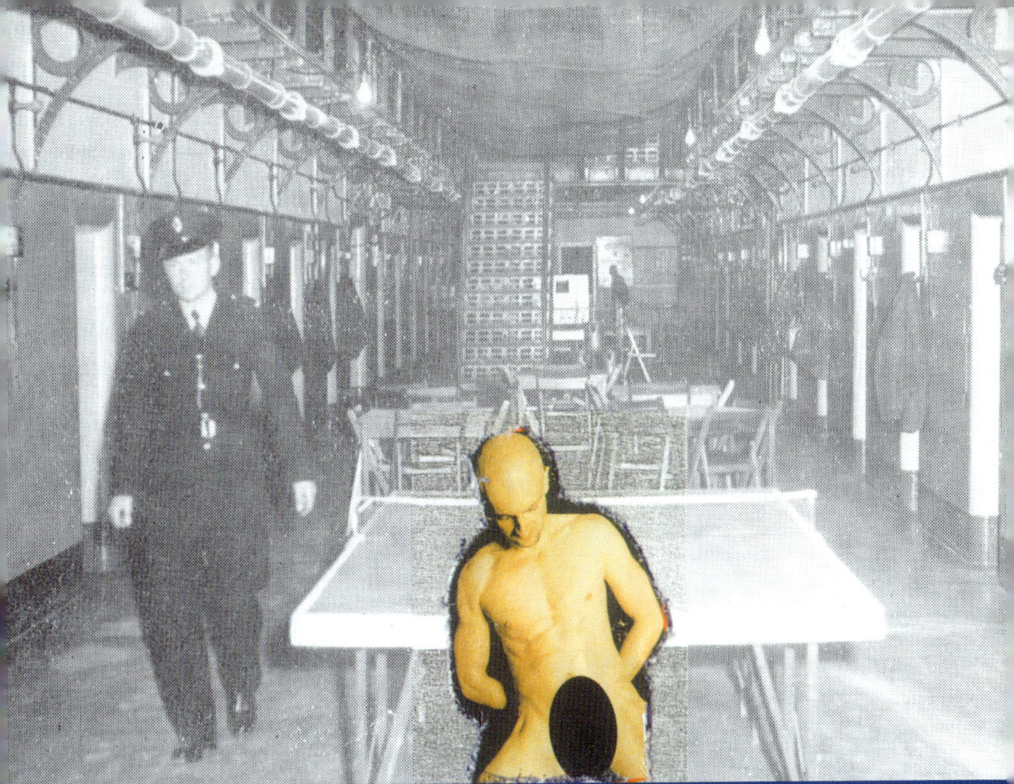

Just coming in first association: still feeling like an idiot and lonely. Feels like everyone's staring at him, as if he's naked.

Calls
a
listener
at
2:30
in
the
morning...

The listener comes to see what the problem is.

the next mor

ing . **Induction**

with the other new people.

650

Eating prison food is horrible.

back in court for sentencing

in front of the judge.

{gets 11 years for murder}

I wish
I was
somewhere
else

He dreams of being somewhere else.
in prison...

2 years 4 months later...

everyone finds out he's in for murder and gives him a hard time,

waits for parole and then gets knocked back,

Works on his education.

{doing something constructive with his time}

After a year and a half he sits his exams

and passes his GCSEs.

He finishes his sentence

and thinks at least
he got some
City and Guilds
out of it

and
now
he
gets
on
with
his
life!

He leaves prison after 11 years and has just missed the wagon...and starts thinking about the last eleven years.

HOW TO SPOT

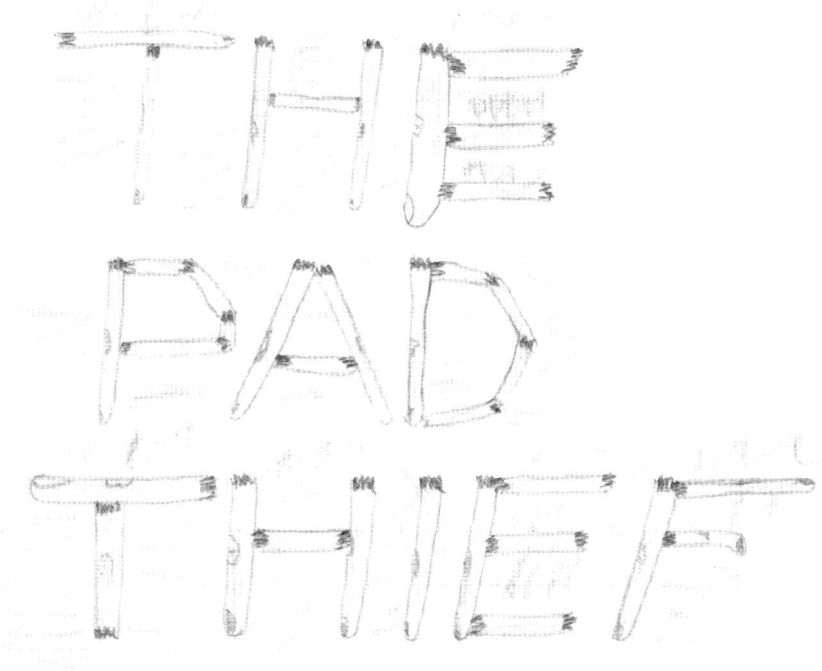

I am the pad thief, I have always got baccy, it's not mine, but yours.
Would you like a rolly? It's not mine it's yours.

He thinks he's clever,
He thinks he's quick.
Oh dear he's lost he's finger tips.

LEWES CROWN COURT

I went to Lewes crown court and received 18 months for aggravated vehicle taking.

I was a fool to myself because I already had a suspended sentence supervision order for burglary and possession of an offensive weapon. The original charge I messed up after just six weeks and ended back at Lewes crown court.

My mum was in court and she was very upset to see them take me away, it also hurt me to see my mum and girlfriend like that. I was very nervous when they took me to the cells and I smoked a lot to steady myself.

You could not show the other prisoners there that you were worried a bit about being in prison or they would try and take the piss out of you.

Also I was a bit pissed off about how far they had shipped me out, they had shipped me out three hundred miles from my home town of Hastings.

So I only get a visit once a month from my mum, girlfriend and my dad.

This is my first time in prison;
hate it,
it’s boring.
What's in the food?
Tastes like crap.
Not enough money,
the mattress is thin,
the pillow is like a breeze block,
bars on the windows,
cold cells,
slamming doors,
noisy when you try to sleep,
miserable screws,
visits once a week,
strip search,
piss test,
level warnings,
cell spins,
wearing other people's clothes,
used people's sheets.

JACK'S STORY

By Danny & Simon

Illustrated by Sheena Best

Jack Harding left home at 16. He couldn't stand listening to his parents arguing any more.

He started a new life, a good life, by renting a bedsit away from all the stress.

One day he set off for an interview for a job he really wanted. Things were looking good.

As he opened the front door he couldn't believe his eyes when he saw two men running off!

He quickly realised the two men had crashed a stolen car.

Here was his chance to prove himself.

Maybe he'd get a cash reward.

Jack took off his coat and had a fight with the two men. What he didn't realise was that they were the wrong men....They were actually on their way to a vicar's convention.

Two Days Later

At home...

At the same time...

When the police arrived Jack tried to explain, but they arrested him.

The police took Jack for an interview and charged him with assault.

Jack went up in front of a judge and was remanded for two weeks.

They put Jack into a police cell.

Jack was taken to the local prison in a sweatbox.

The sweatbox arrived at the front gates of the local prison.
sdbest

A nasty screw greeted Jack.

Arriving at reception Jack was strip searched and shown to a cell.

Jack looked out the window of his new home.

Jack sat on his bunk, and thought about the events that led up to him being in prison and wished that he was back in his bedsit.

Two weeks later Jack was taken back to court in a sweatbox.

The judge passed a sentence of 50 hours community service and Jack was a free man.

Jack ended up washing the windows of his parents house.

HOW TO SPOT A...

BAD PAD MATE

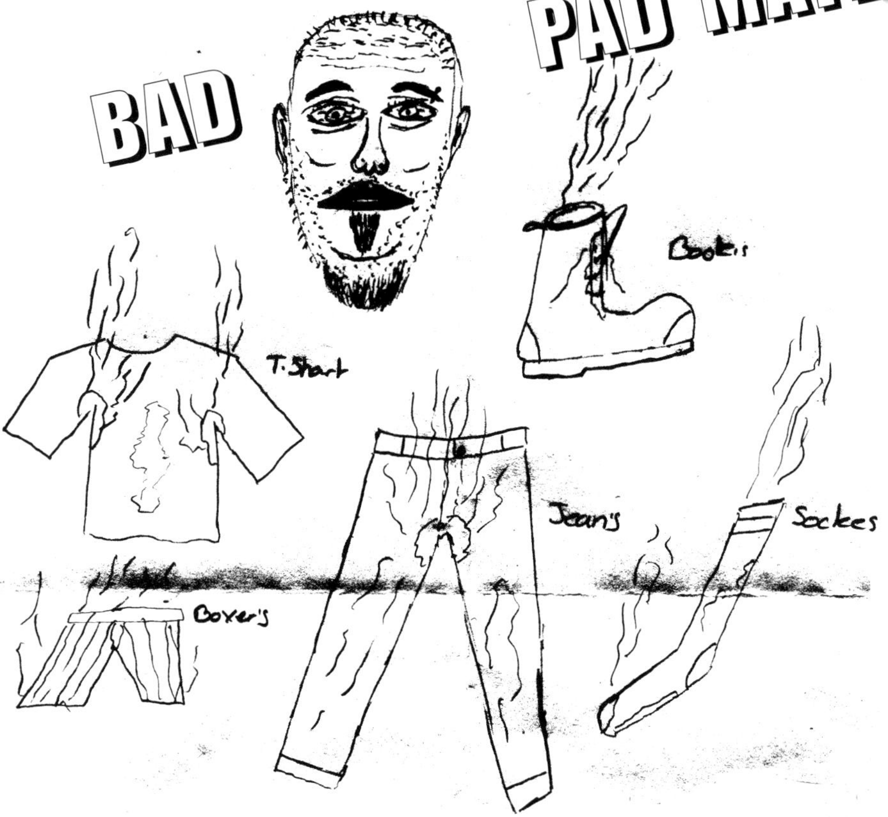

SWEATY FEET BAD BREATH SNORES RELIGIOU

The bad pad mate is always stinking.
He never showers or washes.
He will never change his clothes or bedding.
He will use the loo when you are eating your dinner or he will fart when he goes for a pee.
He will pee all over the loo and the floor.
Plus he never cleans his teeth or ears.
And he never cleans the pad.

Who's got the gear?

Who's got the gear? Got any foil! Who's lending cards? Got any burn!
I've got private cash. I'll sort you out. I've got things inside me. I'll give you double back.
They only paid me two quid. My private cash never went through. They nicked my visit.
My mate didn't come through. Give us a few Blues mate. Sort me the tube. Give us a spliff.
Sort me some pills. I'm a Junkie. You know the score . I'm true mate. I've got fuck all

by Geoff Jenkins

Thank You

Thank you for reading this book of ours. I hope you enjoyed it as much as we did making it. So we all would like to thank all those that gave us the chance to produce a book like this and for giving us the time. This is a book that we are all proud of, so thank you to Simon Heath, Mary Stephenson, Rose Chapman and Sheena Best.

It just goes to prove if you put your mind to it you can do whatever you want, and don't let anyone tell you different. Whatever it is you want to do, go ahead and do it. We all did, and this book proves it! We also hope that this book has helped you the same way it's helped us, like reading, writing, spelling, and most of all, team work with others.

It is time for us to go, so thanks for everyone who has helped from Simon J, Danny B, Scott P, Damon C, Geoff J, Darren B, Ian G, and myself, Steve S.

contexts was funded by the Regional Arts Lottery Programme and HMP Channings Wood

southwest arts | HM PRISON SERVICE | WRITERS IN PRISON Network Ltd | Funded by THE ARTS COUNCIL OF ENGLAND

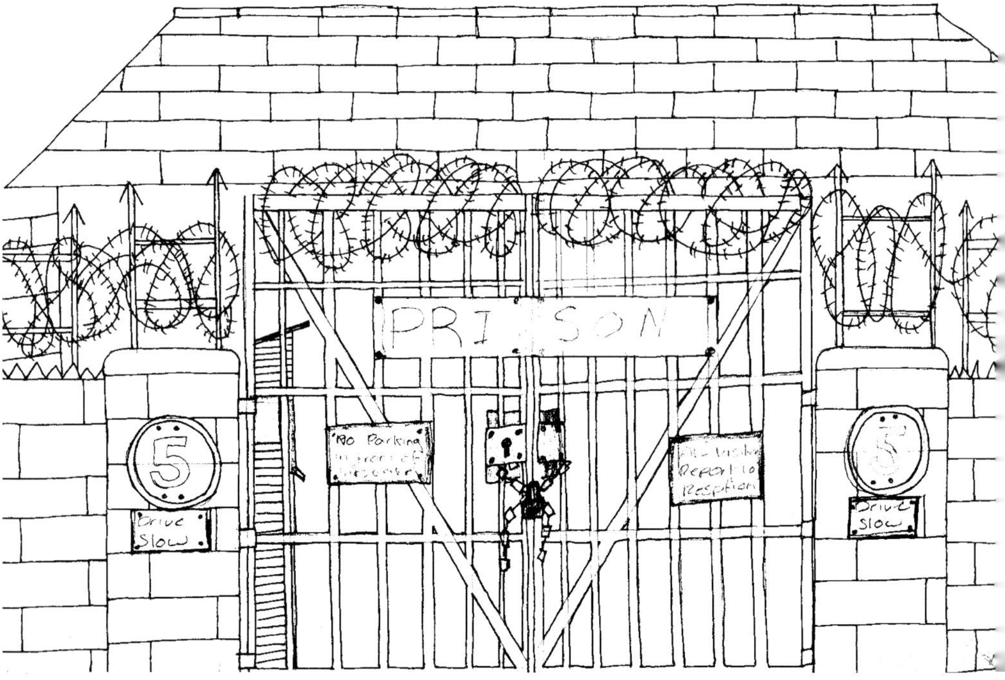